1 batter, 50 pancakes & waffles

Christine France

First published in 2011
LOVE FOOD is an imprint of Parragon Books Ltd

Parragon
Queen Street House
4 Queen Street
Bath BA1 1HE, UK

ISBN: 978-1-4454-3952-5

Printed in China

Written by Christine France
Photography by Clive Bozzard-Hill
Home economy by Valarie Barrett

Notes for the Reader
This book uses both metric and imperial measurements. Follow
the same units of measurement throughout; do not mix metric and
imperial. All spoon measurements are level: teaspoons are assumed
to be 5 ml, and tablespoons are assumed to be 15 ml. Unless
otherwise stated, milk is assumed to be full fat, eggs and individual
vegetables are medium, and pepper is freshly ground black pepper.

The times given are an approximate guide only. Preparation times
differ according to the techniques used by different people and the
cooking times may also vary from those given. Optional ingredients,
variations or serving suggestions have not been included in the
calculations.

Recipes using raw or very lightly cooked eggs should be avoided
by infants, the elderly, pregnant women, convalescents and anyone
suffering from an illness. Pregnant and breastfeeding women are
advised to avoid eating peanuts and peanut products. Sufferers
from nut allergies should be aware that some of the ready-made
ingredients used in the recipes in this book may contain nuts. Always
check the packaging before use.

Contents

Introduction

Who can resist a pile of fresh waffles or pancakes, oozing with syrup or with a tasty topping? Many cultures all over the world celebrate this wonderful dish, with many variations. This book is packed with ideas for waffles, pancakes and crêpes, both sweet and savoury, for any time of day and every occasion, so you can start cooking right now.

The beauty of this book is that every single recipe is based on the Basic Batter Mix (see page 8). To make life easier for you, we have done the hard work so that each recipe is complete and you won't need to refer back to the basic recipe every time.

Equipment

The equipment needed to make the basic batter is all quite standard – a mixing bowl, sieve, measuring jug and spoons, weighing scales and whisk. If you're making pancakes or crêpes, you'll need a large, solid-based frying pan, and for waffle-making you'll need a good-quality waffle iron.

Most waffle makers are electric nowadays, but all cook the batter between two heated, embossed metal plates, making a crisp, golden surface with decorative indentations for holding syrup and other toppings. Most waffle makers make thick, Belgian-style waffles, but some are designed to make thinner, more wafer-like waffles. You can choose one that makes square or circular, or even heart-shaped waffles, and some are marked to make easy divisions in the waffles. Look for one that's easy to clean and has adjustable settings, clear indicator lights or a timer.

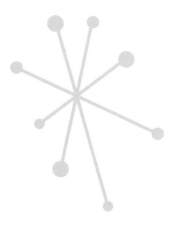

Basic Ingredients

The ingredients for a basic batter are plain flour, baking powder, salt, eggs, milk or other liquid, and oil or butter. Baking powder is omitted when making crêpes.

Plain white flour can be replaced either partly or entirely with other flours, such as wholemeal, rye or buckwheat flour, polenta or gram flour, all giving a different texture and flavour to the finished waffles or pancakes. Cornflour improves crispness, and gluten-free flours, such as rice or potato flour, give a softer, heavier result.

The flour is sifted with baking powder to give a risen, spongy texture to waffles and pancakes, and occasionally it's necessary to add a little bicarbonate of soda to balance the acidity of the mix, as when using buttermilk or yogurt, for instance.

For a sweet batter, sugar is usually added, and this may be any type, depending on the flavour or texture required. Icing and caster sugar dissolve easily and give a light flavour, whereas muscovado and brown sugar add an extra richness of flavour. Honey and maple syrup are more usually used in toppings, but can also be added to the batter mix as a sweetener.

Eggs help to give structure to the mix and these may be used whole, or separated, so that the whites can be whisked to give an extra light texture. Extra egg yolks may be added to enrich the batter.

Milk is used as the liquid for most batters and this can be whole, semi-skimmed or skimmed, or you can use other milks such as coconut, almond or soya milk. Buttermilk, cream or yogurt make a slightly thicker, softer batter with a rich flavour. Fruit juice is used for flavour and to make a light, low-fat batter, and the bubbles in beer help to add lightness. For crêpes, where a thinner batter is required, water is usually added to the mix to make more delicate crêpes.

Salt is added to batters to both sweet and savoury batters, as it helps to strengthen the gluten in the flour, for a light, risen texture.

Flavourings such as vanilla extract or almond extract may be added to the basic batter for a subtle flavour, and these can be replaced with other extracts and essences.

Additional Ingredients

Batters are surprisingly versatile, and once you've mastered the basic mix, you can start experimenting with your own favourite flavours.

Finely chopped, grated or puréed fruits and vegetables not only add flavour to batters, but also boost the nutritional content. Beetroot or spinach will add an appetizing splash of healthy colour to savoury waffles and pancakes. Finely chopped fresh herbs are also great for flavour and add a delicate touch of green to all kinds of batters. Puréed or berry fruits can simply be stirred in for natural sweetness.

Whole grains, nuts and seeds give a crunchy or chewy texture to waffles and pancakes, as well as extra fibre and nutrients.

Spices, both sweet and savoury, are an easy addition to all kinds of batters and can really add a special depth of flavour. Sift the spices with the dry ingredients to ensure even distribution.

A splash of strong coffee makes a good flavouring for many sweet batters, and the flavour combines well with nuts and cream or maple syrup toppings.

Chocoholics can add grated chocolate or chocolate chips to thick batters for waffles and pancakes. Cocoa is used for crêpe batters.

Top Tips

* Waffle and pancake batters benefit from 5 minutes' standing time to allow the raising agent to activate.

* Allow crêpe batters to stand for 15 minutes minimum, so the starch grains absorb moisture.

* Thoroughly preheat the waffle iron or pan before starting to cook.

* Even waffle makers and pans with a non-stick surface need greasing, so always brush or spray with oil or butter before cooking each batch.

* When cooking waffles, have a preheated oven and hot baking sheet ready to keep them hot and crisp.

* Use a ladle or jug to pour the correct amount of batter into the waffle maker or pan, so it's the same each time.

* Don't overfill the waffle compartments; leave room for the batter to expand.

* Avoid stacking waffles until you're ready to serve, to prevent them going soft.

* Interleave crêpes with absorbent kitchen paper to absorb steam while cooking the remaining batter.

* To freeze waffles or pancakes, cool on a wire rack, pack into polythene bags, seal and freeze for up to 3 months.

* To freeze crêpes, cool quickly and interleave with non-stick baking paper, place in a polythene bag, seal and freeze for up to 3 months.

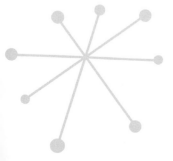

Basic Batter Mix

Makes about 450 ml/16 fl oz batter, enough to make about 8 large waffles, 12 pancakes or 8 crêpes.

* 150 g/5½ oz plain white flour
  (recipes may substitute wholemeal, buckwheat, spelt, or polenta)
* 1½ tsp baking powder (omit from crêpe recipes)
* pinch of salt
* 250 ml/9 fl oz milk
  (recipes may substitute non-dairy milk, such as soya, coconut, etc., buttermilk, yogurt, cream or beer)
* 1 large egg
* 2 tbsp oil or melted butter

This is the basic recipe on which all 50 variations of waffles, pancakes and crêpes in the book are based.

For each recipe the basic mix is highlighted (*) for easy reference, so all you have to do is follow the easy steps each time and you'll never run out of ideas for unusual pancakes, waffles and crêpes.

Please note that the basic ingredients may vary from time to time, so please check these carefully.

Brunch

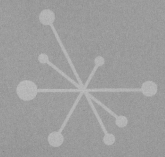

Blueberry Pancakes with Whipped Butter

1. For the whipped butter, place the butter in a bowl and beat with an electric whisk until softened. Add the milk and maple syrup and whisk hard until pale and fluffy.

2. Sift the flour, baking powder, salt and sugar into a bowl. Add the milk, egg, and oil and whisk to a smooth batter. Stir in the blueberries and leave to stand for 5 minutes.

3. Lightly grease a griddle pan or frying pan and heat over a medium heat. Spoon tablespoons of batter onto the pan and cook until bubbles appear on the surface. Turn over with a palette knife and cook the other side until golden brown. Repeat this process using the remaining batter, while keeping the cooked pancakes warm.

4. Serve the pancakes in stacks with extra blueberries, a spoonful of whipped butter and a drizzle of maple syrup.

Serves 4

* 150 g/5½ oz plain white flour
* 1½ tsp baking powder
* pinch of salt
* 2 tbsp caster sugar
* 250 ml/9 fl oz milk
* 1 large egg
* 2 tbsp sunflower oil, plus extra for greasing
* 140 g/5 oz blueberries, plus extra to decorate

Whipped butter

115 g/4 oz unsalted butter, at room temperature

2 tbsp milk

1 tbsp maple syrup, plus extra to serve

Buttermilk Pancakes with Mixed Berry Compôte

1. For the compôte, place the berries, sugar and lemon juice in a saucepan and heat gently until the sugar dissolves. Stir lightly and keep warm.

2. Sift the flour, baking powder, salt and sugar into a bowl. Add the buttermilk, egg and butter and whisk to a smooth batter. Leave to stand for 5 minutes.

3. Lightly grease a griddle pan or frying pan and heat over a medium heat. Spoon tablespoons of batter onto the pan and cook until bubbles appear on the surface. Turn over with a palette knife and cook the other side until golden brown. Repeat this process using the remaining batter, while keeping the cooked pancakes warm.

4. Serve immediately with the compôte.

Serves 4

* 150 g/5½ oz plain white flour
* 1½ tsp baking powder
* pinch of salt
* 1 tbsp caster sugar
* 250 ml/9 fl oz buttermilk
* 1 large egg
* 2 tbsp melted butter
* sunflower oil, for greasing

Compôte
140 g/5 oz raspberries
140 g/5 oz redcurrants
140 g/5 oz blackberries
40 g/1½ oz caster sugar
1 tbsp lemon juice

Silver Dollar Pancakes with Maple Syrup

1. Sift the flour, baking powder and salt into a bowl. Add the buttermilk, egg and butter and whisk to a smooth batter. Leave to stand for 5 minutes.

2. Lightly grease a griddle pan or frying pan and heat over a medium heat. Spoon small spoonfuls of batter onto the pan to make pancakes approximately 4 cm/1½ inches across and cook until bubbles appear on the surface.

3. Turn over with a palette knife and cook the other side until golden brown. Repeat this process using the remaining batter, while keeping the cooked pancakes warm.

4. Serve the pancakes in tall stacks, drizzled with maple syrup.

Serves 4–6

* 150 g/5½ oz plain white flour
* 1½ tsp baking powder
* pinch of salt
* 250 ml/9 fl oz buttermilk
* 1 large egg
* 2 tbsp melted butter
  sunflower oil, for greasing
  maple syrup, to serve

17

Apple & Cinnamon Crêpes

1. Sift the flour, cinnamon and salt into a bowl. Add the milk, apple juice, egg and melted butter and whisk to a smooth, bubbly batter. Leave to stand for 15 minutes.

2. For the filling, place the apples, lemon juice and sugar in a medium-sized saucepan over a medium heat, cover and heat, stirring occasionally, until tender. Keep warm.

3. Put the butter for frying in a 20-cm/8-inch frying pan over a medium heat. Pour in enough batter to just cover the pan, swirling to cover in a thin, even layer. Cook until the underside is golden, then flip or turn with a palette knife and cook the other side until golden brown.

4. Repeat this process using the remaining batter. Interleave the cooked crêpes with kitchen paper and keep warm.

5. Spoon the apples onto the crêpes and fold over into fan shapes. Dust with cinnamon and serve immediately.

Serves 4

* 150 g/5½ oz plain white flour
  1 tsp ground cinnamon, plus extra for dusting
* pinch of salt
* 250 ml/9 fl oz milk
  100 ml/3½ fl oz apple juice
* 1 large egg
* 2 tbsp melted butter
  butter, for frying

Filling
3 dessert apples, peeled and sliced
juice of ½ lemon
2 tbsp golden caster sugar

Banana Pancakes with Whipped Maple Butter

1. Sift the flour, baking powder, sugar and salt into a bowl. Add the buttermilk, egg and butter and whisk to a smooth batter. Mash 2 bananas and mix thoroughly into the batter with the orange rind. Leave to stand for 5 minutes.

2. Lightly grease a griddle pan or frying pan and heat over a medium heat. Spoon tablespoons of batter onto the pan and cook until bubbles appear on the surface.

3. Turn over with a palette knife and cook the other side until golden brown. Repeat this process using the remaining batter, while keeping the cooked pancakes warm.

4. For the maple butter, beat the butter and maple syrup together, whisking until light and fluffy.

5. Slice the remaining banana and serve with the pancakes, with the maple butter spooned over.

Serves 4

- 150 g/5½ oz plain white flour
- 1½ tsp baking powder
- 1 tbsp caster sugar
- pinch of salt
- 250 ml/9 fl oz buttermilk
- 1 large egg
- 2 tbsp melted butter
- 3 ripe bananas
- finely grated rind of 1 small orange
- sunflower oil, for greasing

Maple butter
- 85 g/3 oz butter
- 4 tbsp maple syrup

French Toast Waffles

1. Sift the flour, baking powder, salt, cinnamon and sugar into a bowl. Add the milk, egg and butter and whisk to a smooth batter. Leave to stand for 5 minutes.

2. Lightly grease a waffle maker and heat until hot. Dip the slices of bread quickly into the batter, then place in the waffle maker and cook until golden brown. Repeat, using the remaining batter, while keeping the cooked waffles warm.

3. Serve immediately, with melted butter and sugar.

Serves 4

- 150 g/5½ oz plain white flour
- 1½ tsp baking powder
- pinch of salt
- 1 tsp ground cinnamon
- 2 tbsp caster sugar
- 250 ml/9 fl oz milk
- 1 large egg
- 2 tbsp melted butter, plus extra to serve
- sunflower oil, for greasing
- 8–10 slices brioche-type bread
- demerara sugar, to serve

Chive Waffles with Scrambled Eggs

1. Sift the flour, baking powder and salt into a bowl. Add the milk, egg, butter and chives and whisk to a smooth batter. Leave to stand for 5 minutes.

2. Lightly grease a waffle maker and heat until hot. Pour the batter into the waffle maker and cook until golden brown. Repeat, using the remaining batter, while keeping the cooked waffles warm.

3. For the topping, beat the eggs with the cream and season to taste with salt and pepper. Melt the butter in a medium-sized saucepan over a medium heat and add the egg mixture. Stir over a low heat until the eggs are lightly set but still creamy.

4. Serve immediately, topped with scrambled eggs, garnished with chives and seasoned with extra pepper.

Serves 4

* 150 g/5½ oz plain white flour
* 1½ tsp baking powder
* pinch of salt
* 250 ml/9 fl oz milk
* 1 large egg
* 2 tbsp melted butter
4 tbsp finely chopped chives
sunflower oil, for greasing

Topping
8 eggs
4 tbsp single cream or milk
25 g/1 oz butter
salt and pepper
chives, to garnish

Blinis with Smoked Salmon

1. Sift the flour, baking powder and salt into a bowl. Add the milk, egg yolk, butter and yogurt and whisk to a smooth batter. In a separate bowl, whisk the egg whites to soft peaks and fold lightly and evenly into the batter.

2. Lightly grease a griddle pan or frying pan and heat over a medium heat. Spoon small spoonfuls of batter onto the pan and cook until bubbles appear on the surface.

3. Turn over with a palette knife and cook the other side until golden brown. Repeat this process using the remaining batter to make 30–36 blinis, while keeping the cooked blinis warm.

4. Place a spoonful of crème fraîche on each blini, top with smoked salmon and a sprig of dill and serve warm or cold.

Serves 4

※ 150 g/5½ oz buckwheat flour
※ 1½ tsp baking powder
※ pinch of salt
※ 250 ml/9 fl oz milk
※ 1 large egg, separated
※ 2 tbsp melted butter
  3 tbsp natural yogurt
  1 egg white
  sunflower oil, for greasing

To serve
150 g/5½ oz crème fraîche or
    soured cream
350 g/12 oz smoked salmon
fresh dill sprigs, to garnish

Bacon Waffles with Maple Syrup

1. Sift the flour, baking powder and salt into a bowl. Add the milk, egg and butter and whisk to a smooth batter. Leave to stand for 5 minutes.

2. Lightly grease a waffle maker and heat until hot. Pour the batter into the waffle maker and cook until golden brown. Repeat, using the remaining batter, while keeping the cooked waffles warm.

3. Meanwhile, preheat a grill to high, place the bacon on a grill tray and grill until crisp and golden brown, turning once.

4. Serve the waffles immediately, topped with bacon and drizzled with maple syrup.

Serves 4

* 150 g/5½ oz plain white flour
* 1½ tsp baking powder
* pinch of salt
* 250 ml/9 fl oz milk
* 1 large egg
* 2 tbsp melted butter
  sunflower oil, for greasing
  12 thin slices streaky bacon
  maple syrup, to serve

Pancakes with Baked Mushrooms

1. For the topping, preheat the oven to 200°C/400°F/Gas Mark 6. Beat the butter until softened, stir in the parsley and chives and season to taste with salt and pepper.

2. Mix the garlic and oil together. Place the mushrooms on a baking sheet in a single layer, brush with the garlic oil and sprinkle with salt and pepper to taste. Bake in the oven for about 15 minutes, turning once, until tender.

3. Meanwhile, sift the flour, baking powder and salt into a bowl. Add the milk, egg and butter and whisk to a smooth batter. Leave to stand for 5 minutes.

4. Lightly grease a griddle pan or frying pan and heat over a medium heat. Spoon tablespoons of batter onto the pan and cook until bubbles appear on the surface.

5. Turn over with a palette knife and cook the other side until golden brown. Repeat this process using the remaining batter, while keeping the cooked pancakes warm.

6. Place a mushroom on each pancake, top with a spoonful of herb butter and serve immediately.

Serves 6

* 150 g/5½ oz plain white flour
* 1½ tsp baking powder
* pinch of salt
* 250 ml/9 fl oz milk
* 1 large egg
* 2 tbsp melted butter
  sunflower oil, for greasing

Topping
55 g/2 oz butter
2 tbsp chopped parsley
1 tbsp chopped chives
1 garlic clove, crushed
3 tbsp olive oil
12 field mushrooms
salt and pepper

Everyday

Caramelized Apple Pancakes

1. Sift the flour, baking powder, salt and sugar into a bowl. Add the milk, egg, butter and vanilla extract and whisk to a smooth batter. Leave to stand for 5 minutes.

2. Lightly grease a griddle pan or frying pan and heat over a medium heat. Spoon tablespoons of batter onto the pan and cook until bubbles appear on the surface.

3. Turn over with a palette knife and cook the other side until golden brown. Repeat this process using the remaining batter, while keeping the cooked pancakes warm.

4. For the topping, melt the butter in a medium-size saucepan over a medium heat, then add the apples. Sprinkle with sugar and fry, stirring, for 6–8 minutes, or until softened and golden brown. Stir in the nutmeg.

5. Spoon the apples and juices over the pancakes and serve immediately.

Serves 4

* 150 g/5½ oz plain white flour
* 1½ tsp baking powder
* pinch of salt
* 1 tbsp caster sugar
* 250 ml/9 fl oz milk
* 1 large egg
* 2 tbsp melted butter
* 1 tsp vanilla extract
* sunflower oil, for greasing

Topping
* 70 g/2½ oz butter
* 3 crisp dessert apples, cored and sliced
* 55 g/2 oz caster sugar
* ½ tsp ground nutmeg

Peanut Butter & Jam Waffle Sandwich

1. Sift the flour, baking powder, sugar and salt into a bowl. Add the milk, egg and butter and whisk to a smooth batter. Leave to stand for 5 minutes.

2. Lightly grease a waffle maker and heat until hot. Pour the batter into the waffle maker and cook until golden brown. Repeat this process using the remaining batter, while keeping the cooked waffles warm.

3. Spread half the waffles with peanut butter and the remainder with jam. Sandwich the two together with the peanut butter and jam inside.

4. Dust with icing sugar and serve immediately.

Serves 4

* 150 g/5½ oz plain white flour
* 1½ tsp baking powder
  1 tbsp caster sugar
* pinch of salt
* 250 ml/9 fl oz milk
* 1 large egg
* 2 tbsp melted butter
  sunflower oil, for greasing

Filling
4 tbsp crunchy peanut butter
4 tbsp strawberry jam or raspberry jam
icing sugar, for dusting

Chocolate Chip Pancakes

1. Sift the flour, baking powder, sugar and salt into a bowl. Add the milk, egg and butter and whisk to a smooth batter. Stir in 85 g/3 oz of the chocolate chips and leave to stand for 5 minutes.

2. Lightly grease a griddle pan or frying pan and heat over a medium heat. Spoon tablespoons of batter onto the pan and cook until bubbles appear on the surface.

3. Turn over with a palette knife and cook the other side until golden brown. Repeat this process using the remaining batter, while keeping the cooked pancakes warm.

4. Place the remaining chocolate chips in a bowl and melt over a saucepan of barely simmering water.

5. Stack the pancakes on plates, drizzle with the melted chocolate and serve immediately.

Serves 4

* 150 g/5½ oz plain white flour
* 1½ tsp baking powder
  1 tbsp muscovado sugar
* pinch of salt
* 250 ml/9 fl oz milk
* 1 large egg
* 2 tbsp melted butter
  125 g/4½ oz chocolate chips
  sunflower oil, for greasing

English Pancakes

1. Sift the flour and salt into a bowl. Add the milk, water, egg and butter and whisk to a smooth, bubbly batter. Leave to stand for 15 minutes.

2. Grease a 20-cm/8-inch frying pan with butter and heat over a medium heat. Pour in enough batter to just cover the pan, swirling to cover in a thin, even layer. Cook until the underside is golden, then turn with a palette knife and cook the other side until golden brown.

3. Repeat this process using the remaining batter. Interleave the cooked pancakes with kitchen paper and keep warm.

4. Dust each pancake with sugar, then sprinkle with lemon juice. Roll up and drizzle with golden syrup, if using, and serve immediately.

Serves 4

* 150 g/5½ oz plain white flour
* pinch of salt
* 250 ml/9 fl oz milk
  100 ml/3½ fl oz water
* 1 large egg
* 2 tbsp melted butter
  butter, for frying
  caster sugar, lemon juice and
    golden syrup (optional),
    to serve

15

Potato & Chive Pancakes

1. Sift the flour, baking powder and salt into a bowl. Add the milk, egg and oil and whisk to a smooth batter.

2. Peel the potatoes and grate coarsely, then place in a colander or sieve and sprinkle with salt. Leave to stand for 5 minutes, then press out as much liquid as possible. Stir the grated potato into the batter with the chives, mustard and pepper to taste.

3. Lightly grease a griddle pan or frying pan and heat over a medium heat. Spoon tablespoons of batter onto the pan and cook until bubbles appear on the surface.

4. Turn over with a palette knife and cook the other side until golden brown. Repeat this process using the remaining batter, while keeping the cooked pancakes warm.

5. Serve immediately, with a spoonful of yogurt.

Serves 4

* 150 g/5½ oz plain white flour
* 1½ tsp baking powder
* pinch of salt
* 250 ml/9 fl oz milk
* 1 large egg
* 2 tbsp sunflower oil, plus extra for greasing

225 g/8 oz potatoes

2 tbsp chopped chives

1 tbsp wholegrain mustard

pepper

Greek-style yogurt or soured cream, to serve

Cheese & Bacon Waffles

1. Preheat the grill to high. Place the bacon on a grill rack and grill for 3–4 minutes, turning once, until golden brown and crisp. Drain on kitchen paper, then crumble or chop into small pieces.

2. Sift the flour, baking powder and salt into a bowl. Add the milk, egg and butter and whisk to a smooth batter. Stir in the bacon and cheese and leave to stand for 5 minutes.

3. Lightly grease a waffle maker and heat until hot. Pour the batter into the waffle maker and cook until golden brown. Repeat, using the remaining batter, while keeping the cooked waffles warm.

4. Sprinkle the waffles with grated cheese and serve immediately.

Serves 4

2 thin slices streaky bacon

* 150 g/5½ oz plain white flour
* 1½ tsp baking powder
* pinch of salt
* 250 ml/9 fl oz milk
* 1 large egg
* 2 tbsp melted butter

85 g/3 oz finely grated Cheddar cheese, plus extra for sprinkling

sunflower oil, for greasing

Crêpe Fajitas

1. For the filling, place the beef in a bowl and add the garlic, coriander, cumin, chilli, lime juice and 1 tablespoon of the oil. Cover and leave to chill in the refrigerator for 30 minutes.

2. Sift the polenta, cornflour and salt into a bowl. Add the milk, water, egg and oil and whisk to a smooth batter. Leave to stand for 15 minutes.

3. Lightly grease a 20-cm/8-inch frying pan and heat over a medium heat. Stir the batter and pour in enough to just cover the pan, swirling to cover evenly. Cook until the underside is golden, then flip or turn with a palette knife and cook the other side until golden.

4. Repeat this process using the remaining batter. Interleave the cooked crêpes with kitchen paper and keep warm.

5. To complete the filling, heat the remaining olive oil in a large frying pan over a medium heat, add the red pepper, yellow pepper and onion and fry for 2–3 minutes to soften. Add the beef strips and stir-fry for a further 3–4 minutes, until golden.

6. Spoon the filling onto the crêpes, season to taste with salt and pepper and add a spoonful of soured cream and a spoonful of grated cheese to each. Fold over and serve immediately.

Serves 4

- 150 g/5½ oz medium polenta
- 2 tbsp cornflour
- pinch of salt
- 250 ml/9 fl oz milk
- 100 ml/3½ fl oz water
- 1 large egg
- 2 tbsp corn oil, plus extra for greasing

Filling
- 600 g/1 lb 5 oz sirloin steak or flank steak, cut into thin strips
- 2 garlic cloves, crushed
- 2 tsp ground coriander
- 1 tsp ground cumin
- 1 tsp chilli powder
- juice of 1 lime
- 3 tbsp olive oil
- 1 red pepper, deseeded and sliced
- 1 yellow pepper, deseeded and sliced
- 1 large red onion
- salt and pepper
- soured cream and grated Cheddar cheese, to serve

18

Cannelloni Crêpes

1. Sift the flour and salt into a bowl. Add the milk, water, egg and 2 tablespoons of the olive oil and whisk to a smooth batter. Leave to stand for 15 minutes.

2. Lightly grease a 20-cm/8-inch frying pan and heat over a medium heat. Pour in enough batter to just cover the pan, swirling to cover in an even layer. Cook until the underside is golden, then flip or turn with a palette knife and cook the other side until golden brown.

3. Repeat this process using the remaining batter. Interleave the cooked crêpes with kitchen paper and keep warm.

4. For the filling, heat the olive oil in a frying pan over a medium heat, then add the onion and fry for 2–3 minutes, until softened. Add the turkey and stir-fry for 4–5 minutes, until lightly browned. Add the tomatoes, season to taste with salt and pepper, cover and simmer for 15 minutes. Add the basil.

5. Preheat the oven to 200°C/400°F/Gas Mark 6. Grease a wide ovenproof dish. Fold in 2.5 cm/1 inch on opposite sides of each crêpe. Divide the filling between the crêpes, then roll up and arrange in a single layer in the prepared dish, spooning over the juices.

6. Brush with the remaining olive oil, sprinkle with cheese and bake in the preheated oven for 25–30 minutes, until golden. Serve immediately.

Serves 4

* 150 g/5½ oz plain white flour
* pinch of salt
* 250 ml/9 fl oz milk
  50 ml/2 fl oz water
* 1 large egg
* 4 tbsp olive oil
  sunflower oil, for greasing
  6 tbsp freshly grated Parmesan cheese

Filling
2 tbsp olive oil
1 large onion, sliced
500 g/1 lb 2 oz minced turkey
400 g/14 oz canned chopped tomatoes
3 tbsp chopped fresh basil
salt and pepper

19

Parmesan Crêpe Wraps with Spinach & Walnuts

1. Sift the flour and salt into a bowl. Add the milk, water, egg and butter and whisk to a smooth batter. Stir in the cheese and leave to stand for 15 minutes.

2. Lightly grease a 20-cm/8-inch frying pan and heat over a medium heat. Whisk the batter lightly and pour in enough to just cover the pan, swirling to cover in a thin, even layer. Cook until the underside is golden, then flip or turn with a palette knife and cook the other side until golden brown.

3. Repeat this process using the remaining batter. Interleave the cooked crêpes with kitchen paper and keep warm.

4. For the filling, place the spinach, celery, apple and walnuts in a bowl and toss together. Whisk together the oil, vinegar, and salt and pepper to taste and toss into the salad.

5. Divide the salad between the crêpes, fold over and serve immediately.

Serves 4

* 150 g/5½ oz plain white flour
* pinch of salt
* 250 ml/9 fl oz milk
  50 ml/2 fl oz water
* 1 large egg
* 2 tbsp melted butter
  40 g/1½ oz Parmesan cheese, finely grated
  sunflower oil, for greasing

Filling
100 g/3½ oz baby spinach leaves
2 sticks celery, chopped
1 dessert apple, thinly sliced
55 g/2 oz walnuts, chopped
2 tbsp walnut oil
1 tbsp white wine vinegar
salt and pepper

20

Crêpe Tagliatelle with Seafood Sauce

① Sift the flour and salt into a bowl. Add the milk, water, egg and oil and whisk to a smooth, bubbly batter. Leave to stand for 15 minutes.

② Lightly grease a 20-cm/8-inch frying pan and heat over a medium heat. Pour in enough batter to just cover the pan, swirling to cover in a fairly thin, even layer. Cook until the underside is golden, then flip or turn with a palette knife and cook the other side until golden brown.

③ Repeat this process using the remaining batter. Interleave the cooked crepes with kitchen paper and keep warm. When you have used all the batter, roll up the crêpes and cut into 1 cm/½ inch thick slices.

④ For the sauce, melt the butter in a large frying pan over a medium heat, then add the shallots and fry for 3–4 minutes, until softened. Add the mussels, prawns and lemon juice and stir until thoroughly heated. Stir in the crème fraîche and season to taste with salt and pepper.

⑤ Heat the sauce until almost boiling, then add the sliced crêpes and lightly toss to mix. Sprinkle with the parsley and lemon zest and serve immediately.

Serves 4

✳ 150 g/5½ oz plain white flour
✳ pinch of salt
✳ 250 ml/9 fl oz milk
  50 ml/2 fl oz water
✳ 1 large egg
✳ 2 tbsp sunflower oil,
   plus extra for greasing

Seafood sauce
15 g/½ oz butter
2 shallots, thinly sliced
250 g/9 oz cooked shelled
   mussels
250 g/9 oz cooked peeled
   prawns
juice of 1 lemon
175 g/6 oz crème fraîche
salt and pepper
chopped parsley and lemon
   zest, to garnish

Indulgent

21

Brownie Waffles

1. Sift the flour, baking powder, salt, bicarbonate of soda, cocoa, sugar and cinnamon into a bowl. Add the milk, egg, butter, cream and vanilla extract and whisk to a smooth batter. Stir in the chocolate chips and chopped nuts and leave to stand for 5 minutes.

2. Lightly grease a waffle maker and heat until hot. Pour the batter into the waffle maker and cook until crisp and browned. Repeat, using the remaining batter, while keeping the cooked waffles warm.

3. Serve immediately, with the whipped cream and sprinkled with a few nuts.

Serves 4

* 150 g/5½ oz plain white flour
* 1½ tsp baking powder
* pinch of salt
  ½ tsp bicarbonate of soda
  25 g/1 oz cocoa powder
  55 g/2 oz caster sugar
  1 tsp ground cinnamon
* 250 ml/9 fl oz milk
* 1 large egg
* 2 tbsp melted butter
  3 tbsp double cream
  1 tsp vanilla extract
  85 g/3 oz chocolate chips
  40 g/1½ oz pecan nuts, chopped, plus extra, to serve
  sunflower oil, for greasing
  whipped cream, to serve

22

Sugar Plum Pancakes

1. For the topping, cut the plums into wedges. Melt the butter in a wide saucepan over a high heat, then add the plums and fry for 2–3 minutes. Stir in the sugar and cook over a medium heat, stirring occasionally, until syrupy and slightly caramelized. Keep warm while making the pancakes.

2. Sift the flour, baking powder, salt, sugar and ginger into a bowl. Add the cream, water, egg and butter and whisk to a smooth batter. Leave to stand for 5 minutes.

3. Lightly grease a griddle pan or frying pan and heat over a medium heat. Spoon tablespoons of batter onto the pan and cook until bubbles appear on the surface.

4. Turn over with a palette knife and cook the other side until golden brown. Repeat this process using the remaining batter, while keeping the cooked pancakes warm.

5. Serve warm, with the plums and syrup spooned over the pancakes.

Serves 4

* 150 g/5½ oz plain white flour
* 1½ tsp baking powder
* pinch of salt
  1 tbsp caster sugar
  1 tsp ground ginger
* 250 ml/9 fl oz single cream
  2 tbsp water
* 1 large egg
* 2 tbsp melted butter
  sunflower oil, for greasing

Topping
500 g/1 lb 2 oz red plums, halved and stoned
70 g/2½ oz butter
85 g/3 oz demerara sugar

Banoffee Crêpes

1. Sift the flour and salt into a bowl. Add the milk, coffee, egg and butter and whisk to a smooth, bubbly batter. Leave to stand for 15 minutes.

2. For the filling, put the condensed milk and 4 tablespoons of the cream in a heavy-based saucepan over a low heat and stir until boiling. Cook over a medium heat, stirring continuously, until the mixture starts to caramelize and turns a pale golden brown in colour. Remove from the heat and keep warm.

3. Grease a 20-cm/8-inch frying pan and heat over a medium heat. Pour in enough batter to just cover the pan, swirling to cover in a fairly thin, even layer. Cook until the underside is golden, then flip or turn with a palette knife and cook the other side until golden brown.

4. Repeat this process using the remaining batter. Interleave the cooked crêpes with kitchen paper and keep warm.

5. Spoon the caramel onto the crêpes, slice the bananas and arrange on top, then fold the crêpes over.

6. Whip the remaining cream until just holding its shape, then spoon over the crêpes, sprinkle with grated chocolate and serve.

Serves 4

* 150 g/5½ oz plain white flour
* pinch of salt
* 250 ml/9 fl oz milk
  100 ml/3½ fl oz strong cold black coffee
* 1 large egg
* 2 tbsp melted butter
  butter, for greasing

Filling
400 ml/14 fl oz condensed milk
300 ml/10 fl oz double cream
3 bananas
25 g/1 oz coarsely grated plain chocolate, to serve

24

Lemon Cheesecake Waffles

1. For the filling, beat the cheese, icing sugar, lemon rind and juice together until smooth.

2. Sift the flour, baking powder, salt, caster sugar and ginger into a bowl. Add the milk, egg and butter and whisk to a smooth batter. Leave to stand for 5 minutes.

3. Lightly grease a waffle maker and heat until hot. Pour the batter into the waffle maker and cook until golden brown. Repeat, using the remaining batter, leaving the cooked waffles to cool.

4. Spread half the waffles with the lemon cheesecake filling and sandwich together with the remainder. Top with a spoonful of crème fraîche, sprinkle with macadamia nuts and lemon zest curls and serve.

Serves 4

* 150 g/5½ oz plain white flour
* 1½ tsp baking powder
* pinch of salt
  2 tbsp caster sugar
  1 tsp ground ginger
* 250 ml/9 fl oz milk
* 1 large egg
* 2 tbsp melted butter
  sunflower oil, for greasing

Filling & topping
350 g/12 oz full-fat soft cheese
4 tbsp icing sugar
finely grated rind and juice of
   1 lemon
4 tbsp crème fraîche
55 g/2 oz macadamia nuts,
   chopped and toasted,
   and curls of lemon zest,
   to decorate

25

Ice Cream Crêpes with Berry Compôte

① Sift the flour, salt and sugar into a bowl. Add the milk, water, egg, butter and brandy and whisk to a smooth, bubbly batter. Leave to stand for 15 minutes.

② Meanwhile, for the filling, place the blueberries and raspberries in a small saucepan with the maple syrup. Heat gently until the juices run, then remove from the heat and keep warm.

③ Grease a 20-cm/8-inch frying pan and heat over a medium heat. Pour in enough batter to just cover the pan, swirling to cover in a fairly thin, even layer. Cook until the underside is golden, then flip or turn with a palette knife and cook the other side until golden brown.

④ Repeat this process using the remaining batter. Interleave the cooked crêpes with kitchen paper and keep warm.

⑤ Scoop the ice cream onto the crêpes and fold over. Spoon the berries and syrup on top and serve immediately.

Serves 4

✳ 150 g/5½ oz plain white flour
✳ pinch of salt
1 tbsp icing sugar
✳ 250 ml/9 fl oz milk
100 ml/3½ fl oz water
✳ 1 large egg
✳ 2 tbsp melted butter
1 tbsp brandy
butter, for greasing

Filling
100 g/3½ oz blueberries
100 g/3½ oz raspberries
4 tbsp maple syrup
500 g/1 lb 2 oz mixed berry ice cream or raspberry ice cream

Belgian Waffles

1. Sift the flour, baking powder, salt and sugar into a bowl. Add the milk, egg yolks and butter and whisk to a smooth batter. Whisk the egg whites in a clean bowl until soft peaks form, then fold into the batter.

2. Lightly grease a waffle maker and heat until hot. Pour the batter into the waffle maker and cook until golden brown. Repeat, using the remaining batter, while keeping the cooked waffles warm.

3. Whip the cream until thick enough to just hold its shape and spoon into a piping bag fitted with a large star nozzle. Pipe the cream onto the waffles and top with the strawberries. Dust with icing sugar and serve immediately.

Serves 6

* 150 g/5½ oz plain white flour
* 1½ tsp baking powder
* pinch of salt
* 3 tbsp icing sugar
* 250 ml/9 fl oz milk
* 3 large eggs, separated
* 2 tbsp melted butter
* sunflower oil, for greasing
* icing sugar, for dusting

Topping
300 ml/10 fl oz whipping cream
350 g/12 oz strawberries, halved if large

Blue Cheese & Basil Pancakes

1. Sift the flour, baking powder and salt into a bowl. Add the milk, egg, egg yolks, cheese and butter and whisk to a smooth batter. Leave to stand for 5 minutes.

2. For the basil butter, place all the ingredients in a food processor or blender and process until smooth.

3. Lightly grease a griddle pan or frying pan and heat over a medium heat. Spoon tablespoons of batter onto the pan and cook until bubbles appear on the surface.

4. Turn over with a palette knife and cook the other side until golden brown. Repeat this process using the remaining batter, while keeping the cooked pancakes warm.

5. Top the pancakes with the basil butter and serve immediately.

Serves 4

* 150 g/5½ oz plain white flour
* 1½ tsp baking powder
* pinch of salt
* 250 ml/9 fl oz milk
* 1 large egg
  2 egg yolks
  100 g/3½ oz blue cheese, mashed
* 2 tbsp melted butter
  sunflower oil, for greasing

Basil butter
large handful of fresh basil
140 g/5 oz butter, softened
juice of ½ lemon
1 garlic clove, crushed

28

Beer Waffles with Ham & Cheese

1. Sift the flour, baking powder, salt and mustard powder into a bowl. Add the beer, egg and oil and whisk to a smooth batter. Leave to stand for 5 minutes.

2. Lightly grease a waffle maker and heat until hot. Pour the batter into the waffle maker and cook until golden brown. Repeat, using the remaining batter, while keeping the cooked waffles warm.

3. Preheat the grill to high. Place the waffles on a baking sheet and arrange the ham on top. Sprinkle with grated cheese and grill until melted. Serve immediately.

Serves 4

* 150 g/5½ oz plain white flour
* 1½ tsp baking powder
* pinch of salt
* 2 tsp English mustard powder
* 250 ml/9 fl oz beer or lager
* 1 large egg
* 2 tbsp sunflower oil, plus extra for greasing

Topping
8 thin slices smoked ham

140 g/5 oz Gruyère cheese or Cheddar cheese, coarsely grated

29

Prawn & Garlic Butter Pancakes

1. Sift the flour, baking powder and salt into a bowl. Add the milk, egg and butter and whisk to a smooth batter. Leave to stand for 5 minutes.

2. Lightly grease a griddle pan or frying pan and heat over a medium heat. Spoon tablespoons of batter onto the pan and cook until bubbles appear on the surface.

3. Turn over with a palette knife and cook the other side until golden brown. Repeat this process using the remaining batter, while keeping the cooked pancakes warm.

4. For the prawn and garlic butter, heat the butter in a medium-sized saucepan until melted, add the garlic and prawns and stir for 2–3 minutes, until the prawns turn evenly pink. Add the lemon juice and parsley and season to taste with salt and pepper.

5. Spoon the prawn and garlic butter over the pancakes and serve immediately.

Serves 4

* 150 g/5½ oz plain white flour
* 1½ tsp baking powder
* pinch of salt
* 250 ml/9 fl oz milk
* 1 large egg
* 2 tbsp melted butter
  sunflower oil, for greasing

Prawn & garlic butter
100 g/3½ oz butter
2 garlic cloves, crushed
400 g/14 oz raw peeled tiger prawns
1 tbsp lemon juice
2 tbsp chopped parsley
salt and pepper

30

Fried Waffle Sandwich

1. Sift the flour, baking powder and salt into a bowl. Add the milk, egg and butter and whisk to a smooth batter. Leave to stand for 5 minutes.

2. Lightly grease a waffle maker and heat until hot. Pour the batter into the waffle maker and cook until golden brown. Repeat, using the remaining batter, while keeping the cooked waffles warm.

3. Slice or break up the mozzarella and divide between half the waffles. Top with basil leaves and season to taste with salt and pepper. Place another waffle on top of each.

4. Heat a shallow depth of oil in a frying pan over a high heat until very hot. Quickly dip the waffle sandwiches into the beaten egg, coating on both sides, then lower carefully into the oil and fry for about 30 seconds on each side, until golden and crisp.

5. Drain the waffles on kitchen paper and serve immediately.

Serves 4

* 150 g/5½ oz plain white flour
* 1½ tsp baking powder
* pinch of salt
* 250 ml/9 fl oz milk
* 1 large egg
* 2 tbsp melted butter
  olive oil, for greasing and
    frying

To serve
200 g/7 oz mozzarella cheese
25 g/1 oz fresh basil leaves
2 eggs, beaten
salt and pepper

Healthy

31

Wheat & Dairy-free Pancakes with Orange

1. Sift the flour, baking powder and salt into a bowl. Add the milk, egg, oil and orange rind and whisk to a smooth batter. Leave to stand for 5 minutes.

2. For the topping, cut away all the peel and white pith from the oranges and carefully remove the segments, catching the juices in a bowl. Mix the juices with the maple syrup.

3. Lightly grease a griddle pan or frying pan and heat over a medium heat. Spoon tablespoons of batter onto the pan and cook until bubbles appear on the surface.

4. Turn over with a palette knife and cook the other side until golden brown. Repeat this process using the remaining batter, while keeping the cooked pancakes warm.

5. Serve the pancakes warm, with the orange segments and the syrupy juices spooned over.

Serves 4

* 150 g/5½ oz plain white spelt flour
* 1½ tsp baking powder
* pinch of salt
* 250 ml/9 fl oz sweetened soya milk
* 1 large egg
* 2 tbsp sunflower oil, plus extra for greasing
  finely grated rind 1 orange

Topping
2 large oranges
3 tbsp maple syrup

32

Yogurt Waffles with Poached Apricots

1. For the topping, place the apricots in a saucepan with the apple juice and honey. Bring to the boil, stirring, then reduce the heat to low and cook gently for 10–15 minutes or until tender.

2. Meanwhile, sift the two types of flour, baking powder and salt into a bowl, adding back any bran from the sieve. Add the yogurt, egg and oil and whisk to a smooth batter. Leave to stand for 5 minutes.

3. Lightly grease a waffle maker and heat until hot. Pour the batter into the waffle maker and cook until golden brown. Repeat this process using the remaining batter, while keeping the cooked waffles warm.

4. Spoon the apricots and juices over the waffles and serve immediately.

Serves 4

75 g/2¾ oz plain white flour

75 g/2¾ oz plain wholemeal flour

❋ 1½ tsp baking powder

❋ pinch of salt

❋ 250 ml/9 fl oz low-fat natural yogurt

❋ 1 large egg

❋ 2 tbsp sunflower oil, plus extra for greasing

Topping
400 g/14 oz fresh apricots, stoned and halved

4 tbsp apple juice

1 tbsp honey

Peach-filled Cranberry Crêpes

1. Sift the flour and salt into a bowl. Add the milk, cranberry juice, egg and oil and whisk to a smooth, bubbly batter. Leave to stand for 15 minutes.

2. Meanwhile, for the filling, halve, stone and chop the peaches. Place in a medium-sized saucepan with the cranberry juice and heat over a medium heat until boiling, then remove from the heat and keep warm.

3. Lightly grease a 20-cm/8-inch frying pan and heat over a medium heat. Pour in enough batter to just cover the pan, swirling to cover in a thin, even layer. Cook until the underside is golden, then flip or turn with a palette knife and cook the other side until golden brown.

4. Repeat this process using the remaining batter. Interleave the cooked crêpes with kitchen paper and keep warm.

5. Divide the peaches between the crêpes and top each crêpe with a spoonful of yogurt. Fold over into fan shapes and serve immediately, with the peach juices spooned over.

Serves 4

* 150 g/5½ oz plain white flour
* pinch of salt
* 250 ml/9 fl oz semi-skimmed milk
* 100 ml/3½ fl oz cranberry juice
* 1 large egg
* 2 tbsp sunflower oil, plus extra for greasing

Filling
4 ripe peaches or nectarines
3 tbsp cranberry juice
150 g/5½ oz natural low-fat yogurt

34

Multigrain Pancakes

1. Sift the two types of flour, baking powder and salt into a bowl, tipping in any bran left in the sieve. Add the buttermilk, egg, oil and honey and whisk to a smooth batter. Stir in the oats and seeds and leave to stand for 5 minutes.

2. Lightly grease a griddle pan or frying pan and heat over a medium heat. Spoon tablespoons of batter onto the pan and cook until bubbles appear on the surface.

3. Turn over with a palette knife and cook the other side until golden brown. Repeat this process using the remaining batter, while keeping the cooked pancakes warm.

4. Pour the agave syrup over the pancakes, sprinkle with pumpkin seeds and serve immediately.

Serves 4

75 g/2¾ oz plain white flour

75 g/2¾ oz plain wholemeal flour

✳ 1½ tsp baking powder

✳ pinch of salt

✳ 250 ml/9 fl oz buttermilk

✳ 1 large egg

✳ 2 tbsp sunflower oil, plus extra for greasing

1 tbsp clear honey

40 g/1½ oz porridge oats

2 tbsp sunflower seeds

2 tbsp pumpkin seeds, plus extra to decorate

1 tbsp sesame seeds

agave syrup or maple syrup, to serve

35

Spinach Crêpe Pockets

1. Sift the two types of flour and the salt into a bowl, tipping in any bran left in the sieve. Add the milk, water, egg, oil and spinach and whisk to a smooth, bubbly batter. Leave to stand for 15 minutes.

2. Lightly grease a 20-cm/8-inch frying pan and heat over a medium heat. Pour in enough batter to just cover the pan, swirling to cover evenly. Cook until the underside is golden, then flip or turn with a palette knife and cook the other side until golden brown.

3. Use the remaining batter to make 8 crêpes. Interleave the cooked crêpes with kitchen paper and keep warm. Preheat the oven to 220°C/425°F/Gas Mark 7.

4. For the filling, place the olive spread, flour and milk in a saucepan over a medium heat and, using a hand whisk, whisk until boiling. Cook for a further 2 minutes, stirring, until thickened and smooth.

5. Stir in the tuna, sweetcorn, onion, and salt and pepper to taste. Spoon the filling into the centre of each crêpe and fold over the sides to make a parcel.

6. Place the parcels in an ovenproof dish, joins underneath. Brush lightly with oil and bake in the preheated oven for about 10 minutes, until bubbling. Serve immediately.

Serves 8

75 g/2¾ oz plain white flour

75 g/2¾ oz plain wholemeal flour

pinch of salt

250 ml/9 fl oz skimmed milk

4 tbsp water

1 large egg

2 tbsp olive oil, plus extra for brushing and greasing

70 g/2½ oz cooked spinach, finely chopped

Filling

25 g/1 oz olive spread

25 g/1 oz plain white flour

250 ml/9 fl oz skimmed milk

375 g/13 oz canned tuna, drained and flaked

340 g/11¾ oz canned sweetcorn, drained

1 small red onion, grated

salt and pepper

36

Vegetarian Waffles

1. Sift the two types of flour, baking powder and salt into a bowl, tipping in any bran left in the sieve. Add the milk, egg and oil and whisk to a smooth batter. Stir in the coriander and leave to stand for 5 minutes.

2. Lightly grease a waffle maker and heat until hot. Pour the batter into the waffle maker and cook until golden brown. Repeat, using the remaining batter, while keeping the cooked waffles warm.

3. For the topping, heat the groundnut oil and sesame oil in a wok over a high heat, then add the tofu and gently stir-fry until golden brown. Remove and keep hot. Add the onion, ginger, garlic and broccoli to the wok and stir-fry for 3–4 minutes until tender. Stir in the tamari, then spoon over the waffles.

4. Serve immediately with extra tamari.

Serves 4

75 g/2¾ oz plain white flour

75 g/2¾ oz plain wholemeal flour

1½ tsp baking powder

pinch of salt

250 ml/9 fl oz soya milk

1 large egg

2 tbsp groundnut oil, plus extra for greasing

3 tbsp chopped coriander

Topping

2 tbsp groundnut oil

1 tbsp sesame oil

350 g/12 oz firm tofu, cut into 1-cm/½-inch cubes

1 onion, thinly sliced

1 tbsp finely chopped fresh ginger

1 garlic clove, thinly sliced

250 g/9 oz broccoli, cut into small florets

1 tbsp tamari or soy sauce, plus extra to serve

37

Wild Rice Pancakes with Guacamole

1. Sift the flour, baking powder and salt into a bowl. Add the milk, egg and oil and whisk to a smooth batter. Stir in the rice and leave to stand for 5 minutes.

2. For the guacamole, halve and stone the avocados and scoop out the flesh. Mash with a fork and stir in the lime juice, garlic, tomatoes and chilli. Season to taste with salt and pepper.

3. Lightly grease a griddle pan or frying pan and heat over a medium heat. Spoon tablespoons of the batter onto the pan and cook until bubbles appear on the surface.

4. Turn or flip over with a palette knife and cook the other side until golden brown. Repeat this process using the remaining batter, while keeping the cooked pancakes warm.

5. Serve immediately with the guacamole.

Serves 4

- 150 g/5½ oz plain white flour
- 1½ tsp baking powder
- pinch of salt
- 250 ml/9 fl oz skimmed milk
- 1 large egg
- 2 tbsp sunflower oil, plus extra for greasing
- 140 g/5 oz cooked wild rice

Guacamole
2 ripe avocados
2 tbsp lime juice
1 garlic clove, crushed
2 tomatoes, chopped
1 small red chilli, deseeded and finely chopped
salt and pepper

38

Spiced Crêpes with Watermelon & Feta

① Sift the flour, salt and spices into a bowl. Add the milk, water, egg and butter and whisk to a smooth, bubbly batter. Leave to stand for 15 minutes.

② Lightly grease a 20-cm/8-inch frying pan and heat over a medium heat. Pour in enough batter to just cover the pan, swirling to cover in a fairly thin, even layer. Cook until the underside is golden, then flip or turn with a palette knife and cook the other side until golden brown.

③ Repeat this process using the remaining batter. Interleave the cooked crêpes with kitchen paper and keep warm.

④ Divide the watercress, watermelon and cheese between the crêpes, sprinkle with mint, fold over and serve immediately.

Serves 4

❊ 150 g/5½ oz gram flour
❊ pinch of salt
½ tsp turmeric
½ tsp chilli powder
❊ 250 ml/9 fl oz skimmed milk
100 ml/3½ fl oz water
❊ 1 large egg
❊ 2 tbsp melted butter
sunflower oil, for greasing

Filling
1 bunch watercress
½ small watermelon, cut in quarters lengthwise and sliced
200 g/7 oz feta cheese, crumbled
chopped mint, for sprinkling

Chilli Bean Crêpes

1. Sift the two types of flour and the salt into a bowl, tipping in any bran left in the sieve. Add the milk, tomato juice, egg and oil and whisk to a smooth, bubbly batter. Stir in the parsley and leave to stand for 15 minutes.

2. For the filling, place the kidney beans and cannellini beans in a large saucepan over a medium heat and add the chillies, garlic and tomatoes. Heat gently until boiling, then reduce the heat, season to taste with salt and pepper and keep warm.

3. Lightly grease a 20-cm/8-inch frying pan and heat over a medium heat. Pour in enough batter to just cover the pan, swirling to cover in a thin, even layer. Cook until the underside is golden, then flip or turn with a palette knife and cook the other side until golden brown.

4. Repeat this process using the remaining batter. Interleave the cooked crêpes with kitchen paper and keep warm.

5. Divide the bean mixture between the crêpes, then roll or fold them over and serve immediately.

Serves 4

75 g/2¾ oz plain white flour

75 g/2¾ oz plain wholemeal flour

✳ pinch of salt

✳ 250 ml/9 fl oz semi-skimmed milk

100 ml/3½ fl oz juice from the canned tomatoes used in the filling (made up with water if necessary)

✳ 1 large egg

✳ 2 tbsp olive oil

2 tbsp finely chopped parsley

sunflower oil, for greasing

Filling

400 g/14 oz canned red kidney beans, drained

400 g/14 oz canned cannellini beans, drained

½ tsp crushed chillies

1 garlic clove, crushed

400 g/14 oz canned chopped tomatoes, drained (juice used in the crêpe batter)

salt and pepper

Waffle Hummus Sandwich

1. For the salsa, mix together the tomatoes, chilli, onion, coriander, lemon juice and oil. Season to taste with salt and pepper and leave to stand for about 30 minutes.

2. Sift the two types of flour, baking powder and salt into a bowl, tipping in any bran left in the sieve. Add the milk, egg and oil and whisk to a smooth batter. Leave to stand for 5 minutes.

3. Lightly grease a waffle maker and heat until hot. Pour the batter into the waffle maker and cook until golden brown. Repeat this process using the remaining batter, while keeping the cooked waffles warm.

4. Spread the waffles with hummus, then sandwich together in pairs with rocket leaves and a spoonful of salsa.

5. Serve immediately, with the remaining salsa.

Serves 4

75 g/2¾ oz plain white flour

75 g/2¾ oz plain wholemeal flour

* 1½ tsp baking powder
* pinch of salt
* 250 ml/9 fl oz semi-skimmed milk
* 1 large egg
* 2 tbsp sunflower oil, plus extra for greasing

200 g/7 oz hummus and a handful of rocket leaves, to serve

Salsa

3 ripe tomatoes, finely diced

1 small red chilli, deseeded and finely chopped

1 small red onion, finely diced

2 tbsp chopped coriander

juice of ½ lemon

1 tbsp olive oil

salt and pepper

Special Occasion

41

Christmas Spiced Pancakes

1. Sift the flour, baking powder, salt and mixed spice into a bowl. Add the milk, egg and butter and whisk to a smooth batter. Stir in the cranberries, mixed peel and nuts and leave to stand for 5 minutes.

2. Lightly grease a griddle pan or frying pan and heat over a medium heat. Spoon tablespoons of batter onto the pan to make oval shapes, and cook until bubbles appear on the surface.

3. Turn over with a palette knife and cook the other side until golden brown. Repeat this process using the remaining batter, while keeping the cooked pancakes warm.

4. For the syrup, place the sugar and water in a small saucepan and heat over a low heat, stirring, until the sugar dissolves. Bring to the boil and boil for 1 minute, then add the rum and vanilla and return to the boil. Remove from the heat.

5. Spoon the syrup over the pancakes and serve immediately.

Serves 4

- 150 g/5½ oz plain white flour
- 1½ tsp baking powder
- pinch of salt
- 1 tsp mixed spice
- 250 ml/9 fl oz milk
- 1 large egg
- 2 tbsp melted butter
- 100 g/3½ oz cranberries, chopped
- 40 g/1½ oz chopped mixed peel
- 25 g/1 oz mixed chopped nuts
- sunflower oil, for greasing

Syrup
- 2 tbsp soft dark brown sugar
- 50 ml/2 fl oz water
- 3 tbsp dark rum
- 1 tsp vanilla extract

42

Strawberry Sticks

1. Sift the flour, salt and sugar into a bowl. Add the milk, water, egg, butter and vanilla extract and whisk to a smooth, bubbly batter. Leave to stand for 15 minutes.

2. Lightly grease a 20-cm/8-inch frying pan and heat over a medium heat. Pour in enough batter to just cover the pan, swirling to cover in a thin, even layer. Cook until the underside is golden, then flip or turn with a palette knife and cook the other side until golden.

3. Repeat this process using the remaining batter. Interleave the cooked crêpes with kitchen paper and keep warm.

4. To serve, sprinkle the crêpes with vanilla sugar, roll up firmly and cut diagonally into 2.5-cm/1-inch thick slices. Thread onto about 12 small bamboo skewers with the strawberries between, arrange on a platter and serve immediately.

Serves 4–6

* 150 g/5½ oz plain white flour
* pinch of salt
* 1 tbsp caster sugar
* 250 ml/9 fl oz milk
* 100 ml/3½ fl oz water
* 1 large egg
* 2 tbsp melted butter
* 1 tsp vanilla extract
* butter, for greasing
* vanilla sugar and fresh strawberries, to serve

Crêpes Suzettes

1. Sift the flour and salt into a bowl. Add the milk, water, egg and butter and whisk to a smooth, bubbly batter. Leave to stand for 15 minutes.

2. Melt ½ teaspoon of the butter in a 20-cm/8-inch frying pan over a medium heat. Pour in enough batter to just cover the pan, swirling to cover in a thin, even layer. Cook until the underside is golden, then flip or turn with a palette knife and cook the other side until golden brown.

3. Repeat this process using the remaining batter. Interleave the cooked crêpes with kitchen paper and keep warm.

4. For the sauce, place the butter and sugar in a wide frying pan over a medium heat and stir until melted. Stir in the orange rind and juice with 2 tablespoons of the liqueur and bring to the boil.

5. Fold the crêpes into quarters and add to the pan, spooning over the sauce until evenly heated.

6. To serve, heat the remaining liqueur in a ladle, pour over the crêpes and set alight. Serve immediately, sprinkled with orange zest and slices of orange.

Serves 4

* 150 g/5½ oz plain white flour
* pinch of salt
* 250 ml/9 fl oz milk
  100 ml/3½ fl oz water
* 1 large egg
* 2 tbsp melted butter, plus extra for greasing
  shreds of orange zest and slices of orange, to decorate

Sauce
100 g/3½ oz butter
100 g/3½ oz caster sugar
finely grated rind and juice of 1 orange
100 ml/3½ fl oz orange liqueur, such as Grand Marnier or Cointreau

Valentine Waffles

1. For the sauce, melt the chocolate with the cream and rum in a bowl over a saucepan of barely simmering water. Stir until smooth, remove from the heat and keep warm.

2. Sift the flour, baking powder and salt into a bowl. Add the milk, egg and oil and whisk to a smooth batter. Leave to stand for 5 minutes.

3. Lightly grease a waffle maker and heat until hot. Pour the batter into the waffle maker and cook until golden brown. Repeat, using the remaining batter, while keeping the cooked waffles warm.

4. Using a heart-shaped cutter approximately 7 cm/2¾ inches in diameter, stamp a heart shape from the centre of each waffle.

5. Serve the waffles on individual plates, with the raspberries in the centre, the chocolate sauce poured around, and the heart-shaped cut-outs on the side.

Serves 4

* 150 g/5½ oz plain white flour
* 1½ tsp baking powder
* pinch of salt
* 250 ml/9 fl oz milk
* 1 large egg
* 2 tbsp sunflower oil, plus extra for greasing

200 g/7 oz raspberries, to serve

Chocolate sauce
100 g/3½ oz plain chocolate
4 tbsp single cream
1 tbsp dark rum or brandy

45

Summer Berry Pancake Stack

1. Sift the flour, baking powder, salt and sugar into a bowl. Add the milk, egg, butter and mint and whisk to a smooth batter. Leave to stand for 5 minutes.

2. Lightly grease a griddle pan or frying pan and heat over a medium heat. Spoon tablespoons of batter onto the pan and cook until bubbles appear on the surface.

3. Turn over with a palette knife and cook the other side until golden brown. Repeat this process using the remaining batter, while keeping the cooked pancakes warm.

4. To serve, stack the pancakes with the yogurt and berries, dust with icing sugar, decorate with mint sprigs and serve immediately.

Serves 4

- 150 g/5½ oz plain white flour
- 1½ tsp baking powder
- pinch of salt
- 1 tbsp caster sugar
- 250 ml/9 fl oz milk
- 1 large egg
- 2 tbsp melted butter
- 2 tbsp finely chopped fresh mint
- sunflower oil, for greasing

To serve

- 200 g/7 oz Greek-style natural yogurt
- 350 g/12 oz mixed berries, such as blackberries, raspberries, redcurrants and blueberries
- icing sugar, for dusting
- fresh mint sprigs, to decorate

Pumpkin & Spice Pancakes

1. Sift the flour, baking powder, sugar, spices and salt into a bowl. Add the milk, egg and butter and whisk to a smooth batter. Stir in the pumpkin and leave to stand for 5 minutes.

2. Lightly grease a griddle pan or frying pan and heat over a medium heat. Spoon tablespoons of batter onto the pan and cook until bubbles appear on the surface.

3. Turn over with a palette knife and cook the other side until golden brown. Repeat this process using the remaining batter, while keeping the cooked pancakes warm.

4. Mix the demerara sugar and mixed spice together and sprinkle over the pancakes, then drizzle with melted butter and serve immediately.

Serves 4

* 150 g/5½ oz plain white flour
* 1½ tsp baking powder
  2 tbsp muscovado sugar
  1 tsp mixed spice
  ½ tsp ground nutmeg
* pinch of salt
* 250 ml/9 fl oz milk
* 1 large egg
* 2 tbsp melted butter, plus extra to serve
  175 g/6 oz cooked pumpkin, mashed
  sunflower oil, for greasing
  2 tbsp demerara sugar and ½ tsp mixed spice, to serve

Cherry Crêpe Baskets

1. Sift the flour and salt into a bowl. Add the milk, orange juice, egg and butter and whisk to a smooth, bubbly batter. Leave to stand for 15 minutes.

2. Lightly grease a 20-cm/8-inch frying pan and heat over a medium heat. Pour in enough batter to just cover the pan, swirling to cover in a fairly thin, even layer. Cook until the underside is golden, then flip or turn with a palette knife and cook the other side until golden brown.

3. Repeat this process using the remaining batter. Interleave the cooked crêpes with kitchen paper and keep warm.

4. Preheat the oven to 200°C/400°F/Gas Mark 6. Place 8–10 small metal pudding moulds on a baking sheet, brush with oil and drape the pancakes over. You can do this in batches.

5. Bake the crêpes in the preheated oven for about 10 minutes, until set into shape. Remove carefully and place on serving plates. Mix the ricotta cheese, sugar, vanilla extract and cherries together and spoon into the baskets.

6. Decorate with whole cherries and serve immediately.

Serves 4

* 150 g/5½ oz plain white flour
* pinch of salt
* 250 ml/9 fl oz milk
  100 ml/3½ fl oz orange juice
* 1 large egg
* 2 tbsp melted butter
  sunflower oil, for greasing
  whole cherries, to decorate

Filling
250 g/9 oz ricotta cheese
2 tbsp icing sugar
1 tsp vanilla extract
350 g/12 oz cherries, stoned

48

Pesto & Parmesan Canapés

1. Sift the flour, baking powder and salt into a bowl. Add the milk, egg, oil and pesto and whisk to a smooth batter. Leave to stand for 5 minutes.

2. Lightly grease a griddle pan or frying pan and heat over a medium heat. Spoon teaspoons of batter onto the pan and cook until bubbles appear on the surface.

3. Turn over with a palette knife and cook the other side until golden brown. Repeat this process using the remaining batter, while keeping the cooked pancakes warm.

4. Place a small dab of pesto on each pancake, top with cheese shavings, garnish with basil sprigs and serve immediately.

Serves 10–12

* 150 g/5½ oz plain white flour
* 1½ tsp baking powder
* pinch of salt
* 250 ml/9 fl oz milk
* 1 large egg
* 2 tbsp sunflower oil, plus extra for greasing
* 3 tbsp red pesto or green pesto, plus extra to serve
* Parmesan cheese shavings, to serve
* fresh basil sprigs, to garnish

Salami Roll-ups

1. Place the water and herbs in a food processor and process until almost smooth. Sift the flour and salt into a bowl. Add the milk, egg, oil and herb liquid and whisk to a smooth, bubbly batter. Leave to stand for 15 minutes.

2. Lightly grease a 23-cm/9-inch frying pan and heat over a medium heat. Pour in enough batter to just cover the pan, swirling to cover in a fairly thin, even layer. Cook until the underside is golden, then flip or turn with a palette knife and cook the other side until golden brown.

3. Repeat this process using the remaining batter. Interleave the cooked crêpes with kitchen paper and keep warm.

4. Mix together the mascarpone cheese and mayonnaise and spread over the crêpes. Arrange the salami slices on top and roll up firmly.

5. Cut the rolls into 2-cm/¾-inch thick slices and spear with a cocktail stick to hold in place. Serve as canapés.

Serves 6–8

100 ml/3½ fl oz water

3 tbsp chopped summer herbs, such as parsley, chives and chervil

150 g/5½ oz plain white flour

pinch of salt

250 ml/9 fl oz milk

1 large egg

2 tbsp olive oil

sunflower oil, for greasing

Filling
100 g/3½ oz mascarpone cheese

3 tbsp mayonnaise

225 g/8 oz salami Milano, thinly sliced

Blue Cheese Waffles

1. Sift the flour, baking powder and salt into a bowl. Add the milk, egg and oil and whisk to a smooth batter. Stir in the blue cheese and leave to stand for 5 minutes.

2. Lightly grease a waffle maker and heat until hot. Pour the batter into the waffle maker and cook until golden brown. Repeat, using the remaining batter, while keeping the cooked waffles warm.

3. Top the waffles with the flaked salmon and horseradish sauce. Season with pepper and serve with the lemon wedges.

Serves 8

* 150 g/5½ oz plain white flour
* 1½ tsp baking powder
* pinch of salt
* 250 ml/9 fl oz milk
* 1 large egg
* 2 tbsp sunflower oil, plus extra for greasing
  100 g/3½ oz blue cheese, crumbled

To serve
225 g/8 oz hot smoked salmon, flaked
4 tbsp horseradish sauce
pepper
lemon wedges